Figure Skating EXPLAINED

A Spectator's Guide to
Competitive Figure Skating

by

S.J. Thomas

Copyright © 2018 by S.J. Thomas

All rights reserved. This book or any portion thereof may not be reproduced or used in any manner whatsoever without the express written permission of the publisher except for the use of brief quotations in a book review.

ISBN13: 978-1-948713-01-6

Triple Toe Press

info@tripletoepress.com
www.tripletoepress.com

Table of CONTENTS

Chapter 1: Watching Figure Skating 1

Chapter 2: Figure Skating Disciplines 3

Chapter 3: The Long Road to Gold 5

Chapter 4: The Basics of Figure Skating Competitions 9
- Spins 9
- Footwork 12
- Jumps 12

Chapter 5: The Competitive Performance 15

Chapter 6: The International Judging System (IJS) 23
- The Technical Element Score (TES) 24

Chapter 7: Grades of Execution (GOE) 31

Chapter 8: Program Component Score (PCS) 37

Chapter 9: Total Competition Score (TCS) 41

Chapter 10: Figure Skating Judges 43
- A Guided Tour Through Judging a Competition 44

Chapter 11: The Winter Olympics 47

Chapter 12: The Fun Stuff 51
- Resources 54
- Photo Credits 55

Chapter 1
Watching Figure Skating

Figure skating is one of the most beautiful athletic sports, yet it is also grueling, dangerous, and extremely competitive. Every four years, hundreds of figure skaters around the world compete at the highest levels of their sport for a chance to represent their country at the Olympics, and dream of winning Olympic Gold. And every four years, millions of viewers watch these events to cheer for their favorite competitors. But watching figure skating can be confusing. What kind of scoring system are they using? Why did the competitor that fell on a jump earn a higher score than the one that didn't? How did the athletes get chosen to be on their Olympic teams? You will find answers to these questions and many more in this book. You will learn about the different jumps, spins, and other elements skaters use in their performances. You will be able to tell the difference between a death spiral and a death drop. You will learn about the International Judging System (IJS), which has been in use for 15 years but is still referred to as the "new" system. You will learn about the long road skaters take to work their way up the competitive ranks for the chance to be the best figure skater in the world. This book will give you all the information you need to get the most enjoyment from watching the beauty and heartbreak of competitive figure skating.

Chapter 2
Figure Skating Disciplines

There are four different disciplines in figure skating that are regularly viewed by fans. Mens and Ladies Singles skating, Pairs skating, and Ice Dance.

Singles Freestyle is the figure skating you see most often. One solo athlete performs a complex routine of jumps, spins, and connecting footwork and movements choreographed to music. Each skater performs a "Short program" with required technical elements, and a "Free Skate" program (formerly and still sometimes called the "long program") that also has required elements of jumps, spins, and footwork, but the skaters have more freedom with regard to the content of the program.

Mens - The men's competition is known for strong jumping. The top men are now expected (although not required) to do at least one 4 rotation ("quad") jump. The first quad, a quad toe loop, was landed in 1988 by Kurt Browning. Over the next ten years several men landed them in competitions, and by 1999 men were attempting multiple quads in their free skate programs. Another decade later, Nathan Chen performed 5 quad jumps in his Free Skate program to win the 2018 US National Championship title and the top spot on the Olympic team.

Ladies - Only one woman has ever landed a quad jump in competition, although there have been several attempts. In 2002 Japan's Miki Ando landed a quadruple salchow at the Junior Grand Prix Final. Since the first one in 1988, only 8 women have successfully landed a triple axel - a 3.5 rotational jump taking off forward and landing backward. However, triple jumps including the difficult triple lutz are expected of the top competitors in the women's competitions. The ladies event is also known for amazing spins with many different, difficult positions and ever-increasing speed, which make them a joy to watch.

Pairs - Pairs skating can be the most spectacular of the skating disciplines. Pairs skating at the senior level require throw jumps, where the male skater throws the female skater into the air during the takeoff of a jump; a twist lift, where the female skater is thrown above the head of the male skater and caught again, and the ominously named death spiral, where the female skater's head is just inches from the ice and her partner's skate blade. Pairs also have requisite side by side jumps and spins that must be done in unison. The pairs team also have a Short program and a Free Skate program with required elements in each. Quad throw jumps and twist jumps are attempted in pairs skating. The first successful quad twist was in 1978 by Marina Cherkasova and Sergei Shakrai of Russia. It was not successfully performed again until 1987 by Ekaterina Gordeeva and Sergei Grinkov of Russia. In 2018, quad lifts and throw jumps are regularly attempted and successfully performed at the top senior levels.

Ice Dance - In ice dance, the emphasis is on edges, flow, unison, speed, grace and style. The teammates cannot be far apart from each other for extended periods of time and need to be skating together most of the time, using dance holds. They also have required lifts, but in ice dance lifts may not be higher than shoulder height. The ice dancers perform two routines, a Short Dance and a Free Dance. They are scored on their depth of edges, correctness of the steps, how closely they skate together, speed, extension, unison, effortlessness and flow.

Chapter 3
The Long Road to Gold

Figure skating in the US is governed by United States Figure Skating. They create and oversee all the rules by which figure skaters test, compete, and become eligible for major national and international competitions. There are eight levels of competitive figure skating in the US. After many years of training and competitions, skaters work their way through the testing levels. The highest level of testing and competition is the Senior level. Those skaters that pass their Senior Moves in the Field test (a test of footwork and edge skills) and the Senior Freestyle test (a test of jumps, spins, footwork and presentation) are eligible to compete in the qualifying events to get to the national level.

The USFS competitive freestyle figure skating categories for Standard Track and Adult Track are:

Standard (Olympic) Track	Adult Track
Pre-preliminary	Adult Pre-Bronze
Preliminary	Adult Bronze
Pre-juvenile	Adult Silver
Juvenile	Adult Gold
Intermediate	
Novice	Adult Intermediate-Novice
Junior	
Senior	Adult Junior-Senior

The Road to the Olympics for Figure Skaters

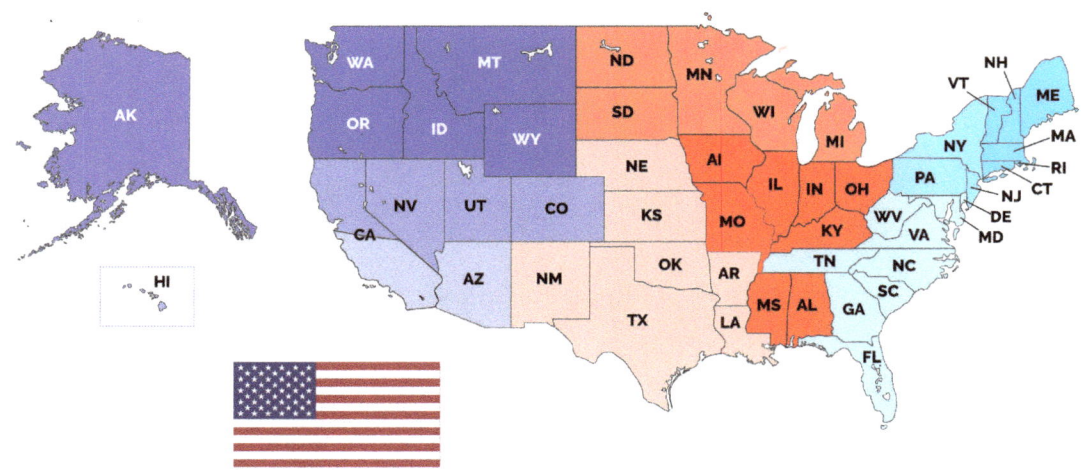

EASTERN SECTION			MIDWESTERN SECTION			PACIFIC COAST SECTION		
New England	**North Atlantic**	**South Atlantic**	**Eastern Great Lakes**	**Upper Great Lakes**	**Southwestern**	**Northwest Pacific**	**Central Pacific**	**Southwest Pacific**
Connecticut Maine Massachusetts New Hampshire Rhode Island Vermont	New Jersey New York Pennsylvania (Erie)	Delaware District of Columbia Florida Georgia Maryland North Carolina Pennsylvania (excluding Erie) South Carolina Virginia West Virginia Chattanooga, Tennessee	Alabama Indiana Kentucky Michigan (Lower Peninsula) Mississippi Ohio Tennessee (excluding Chatanooga)	Illinois Iowa Michigan (Upper Peninsula) Minnesota Missouri (excluding Kansas City and St. Joseph's) North Dakota South Dakota Wisconsin	Arkansas Colorado (excluded for synchronized only) Kansas Louisiana Nebraska New Mexico Missouri (Kansas City and St. Joseph's) Oklahoma Texas	Alaska Idaho Montana Oregon Washington Wyoming	California (all cities north of and including Visalia) Colorado (for synchronized only) Hawaii Nevada Utah	Arizona California (all cities south of Visalia)

Regionals — **9 Geographic Regions** - the top four finishers from each event advance to Sectionals

Sectionals — **3 Geographic Sections** (Eastern, Midwestern, Pacific Coast) - the top four finishers from each event advance to Nationals

National Championships — **1 National Championship.** The top 5 finishers are considered for the World and Olympic teams, and spots are awarded based on this competition and past performances at national and international competitions in the last year.

→ **World Championships** *Every year*

→ **Winter Olympics** *Once every four years*

There are nine geographic regions in the USFS system. Every year in October, USFS Regional competitions are held in each region for singles events. Any skater who has passed the requisite test may compete at his or her level at Regionals. The top 4 finishers for the Senior event are then eligible to compete in one of the three Sectional events, according to their geographical area. Pairs and Ice Dance teams do not have regional events. Their competition season starts at the Sectional level competition. The top four winners at each Sectional event advance to the National championships. In addition, skaters who have placed in the top 5 at the previous Nationals, skaters who have won an Olympic medal at the most recent games, skaters who have won a medal at the previous year's world championships, or skaters who have advanced to the current seasons "Grand Prix Final" (an international skating series competition) may also compete at the US Nationals without attending the Sectional Competition.

At the conclusion of the US National Championship the World and/or Olympic teams are chosen. The athletes are chosen based on several criteria, including their finish at Nationals and their performance at important international competitions over the previous year. The number of teammates for each discipline is chosen based on the number of slots available.

The following, excerpted from the new U.S. Figure Skating document "World Team Selection Procedures," outlines the essence of the new procedure:

Athletes shall be selected based upon performance(s) in the events below. The events have been stratified into tiers from the highest value events in Tier 1 through the lowest value events in Tier 3. Events within each tier shall be evaluated at equal weight.

Tier 1
- 2017 U.S Figure Skating Championships
- 2016 ISU Grand Prix Final
- 2016 ISU World Figure Skating Championships

Tier 2
- 2016 Grand Prix Series Competitions
- 2016 Four Continents Figure Skating Championships

Tier 3
- 2016 Challenger Series Events and other senior international competitions
- 2016 U.S. Figure Skating Championships
- 2016 World Junior Figure Skating Championships
- 2016 ISU Junior Grand Prix Final

The names of the top five athletes/teams at the current U.S. Figure Skating Championships will be automatically placed into the pool of athletes/teams being considered for the World Team, if eligible. Consideration will be given to add additional athletes/teams to the pool by reviewing the events above in priority order and adding others due to extenuating circumstances as approved by the respective International Committee Discipline Group. Discussion on, and the selection of the pool of athletes identified by the International Committee Discipline Group, will be limited to the competitions listed above.

Source: http://www.icenetwork.com/news/2017/01/20/214003280

Chapter 4

The Basics of Figure Skating Competitions

All figure skating programs are a choreographed presentation of spins, jumps and footwork or connecting movements. A skater learns the basics of these movements, and as they progress in skill levels they will add more difficulty for each element. Jumps begin as half-revolution, then full revolution jumps, and progressing, after hundreds and even thousands of hours of training, to multi-rotational jumps and combination jumps (performing one jump right after another). Spins begin as a simple two-foot spin, progress to one-foot spins and then different positions such as sit spin and camel (or arabesque) spins are learned and then done in sequence. Every movement becomes more complex and more difficult as the skater progresses in skill.

Spins

The number of spin variations possible is extraordinary. Skaters are rewarded for creative and innovative spin variations. But the combination of spins is based on several foundational spin elements and variations. For most skaters, this means the forward spins are done on the left foot and the back spins are done on the right foot. In both cases the skater is spinning counterclockwise. However, some skaters jump and spin clockwise, also called "left-handed" or "the other way".

Scratch spin or upright spin - the skater is in a straight up and down position with feet crossed. This can be performed as a forward or a backward (back) spin. This spin is simple in style but can be extremely fast.

Sit spin - the skater's skating leg is bent and the thigh is parallel to the ice. The free leg is held straight out in front. It is imperative that the skating thigh be at least parallel to the ice or the spin will not get credit in the IJS scores.

Broken leg sit spin - a sit spin where the knees are touching, and the free leg is held out to the side.

Pancake sit spin - a sit spin where the free leg is tucked over the skating knee and the body is pressed down flat to the skating thigh.

Cannonball spin - a sit spin where the free leg is held out front and the body is pressed down against the skating thigh.

Camel spin - in the camel spin the skater's skating leg is straight and the free leg is held straight out behind the skater, with the free foot being at hip level or higher.

Layback spin - in a layback spin the skater bends backward at the waist and the back is arched.

Catch-foot spin - a spin where the skater catches the blade of the free foot and brings the skate to some position above the waist, shoulders, or head.

Haircutter spin - a variation of the catch-foot spin where the foot and head are brought together behind the body.

I-spin - an upright spin where the skater holds one foot up to the head in the front rather than the back as in a Biellmann spin. This can be done holding either the ankle or the skate.

Sit spin. Photo credit: Vesperholly, CC BY-SA 2.5

Pancake spin. Photo credit: Luu CC BY-SA 3.0

Haircutter spin. Photo credit: Doug Drew CC BY 3.0

Shotgun spin - another variation of an upright spin where the leg is held straight out in front of the skater.

Biellmann spin - named after Denise Biellmann, the skater grabs the blade of the free foot and brings the foot straight up behind their head.

Back spin - a backspin is a spin that is performed on an outside back edge of the opposite foot than the forward spin. The skater will often change from a front spin to a back spin during their combination spins. This is called a change foot spin. Upright, layback, sit spins, and camel spins can all be performed as either front spins or back spins.

Biellmann spin. Photo credit: David W. Carmichael CC-BY-SA-3.0

Flying sit spin - a variation of the sit spin where the skater enters the spin from a jump.

Flying camel spin - a variation of the camel spin where the skater enters the spin from a jump.

Doughnut spin - a variation of a camel spin where the skater creates a horizontal circle shape with the body by holding the blade of the free leg close to their head.

Death drop spin - the death drop is a type of flying spin where the skater takes off on a forward edge, kicks that leg back and lands in a back sit spin position. The air position is particularly important to discern the death drop from an ordinary flying sit spin.

Death drop. Photo credit: Kevin Rushford CC BY-SA 3.0

Dance spins - ice dance teams also perform dance spins, which can be similar to pair spins. They must be touching or holding each other during the spin but can each be in different positions.

Pair spins - pairs skaters will perform side by side spins of the type described above. They also will do pair spins, where the couple are touching or holding each other and performing the spin together. The skaters can be in the same or in different positions during the spins.

Pairs spin. Photo credit: David W. Carmichael CC-BY-SA 3.0

Footwork

The connecting steps between jump and spin elements is known as footwork. Footwork sequences are a required part of every competitive skating performance. These steps are generally described for the way the skater changes direction and/or skating edge. They can also be used as transitional steps for beauty, elegance, and choreography. Below is a list of common footwork steps:

Change Direction Change Feet	Change Direction Same Foot	Moves for Power and Speed	Moves for Style
Mohawk	Three-turn	Chasses	Twizzles
Choctaw	Rocker	Progressives	Spread Eagle
Toe Steps	Bracket	Crossovers	Ina Bauer
	Counter		Spirals

Jumps

In some ways, jumps are the very heart of figure skating. These jumps are very important to a figure skater's overall program and can be the determining factor for the medal winners in a competition. They can be extremely exciting to watch and devastating when the skater falls or "pops" the jump. "Popping" a jump means that the skater was intending to do a multi-rotation jump and did a single rotation instead.

There are six basic jumps in figure skating. The jumps are different based on the edge of takeoff, the edge of the landing, and whether the toe pick is used as an assist in the air. They are listed here in the relative order of difficulty.

Toe loop - takes off on a back outside edge while using the toe-pick of the opposite foot to lift into the air, turn and land on a back outside of the skating foot.

Salchow - takes off on a back inside edge, swing the leg up and around and through to land on a back outside edge of the opposite foot.

Loop - takes off on a back outside edge, turn in the air and land on the same back outside edge.

Flip - takes off on a back inside edge while using the toe-pick of the opposite foot, turn in the air and land on a back outside edge of the picking foot. The flip jump is NOT a backflip. Backflips are illegal in skating competitions.

Lutz - take off on a back outside edge, pick and land on a back outside edge of the picking foot. This jump is similar to the flip but more difficult because the skater has to rotate in the opposite direction from the outside edge they are traveling on. Judges pay particularly close attention that the skating foot is on the outside edge at the moment of take-off. If the blade switches to an inside edge before take-off it is called as an incorrect edge. This is also referred to as a "flutz".

Axel - forward take off from an outside edge, spin in the air one (or more) and a half revolutions and land on the back outside edge of the opposite foot.

All of these jumps can be done in multiple rotations. Two rotations is a double jump, three rotations is a triple jump, and four rotations is a quad jump. As of January 2018 all of these jumps have been landed as quad with the exception of the axel. Also as of this writing quad jumps are generally performed only by men.

There are also additional jumps that are used for connecting movements and for their beauty and/or excitement.

Half loop - takes off on a back outside edge, jump and land of a back inside edge of the opposite foot. This is often done as an in-between jump in a combination jump. After landing one of the 6 jumps above, the half loop jump will put the skater on the correct edge to perform a salchow or flip jump as a second jump in the combination.

Walley and Toe Walley - takes off on a right back inside edge, rotate once in the air and land on the right back outside edge of the same foot. A toe walley uses the toe pick to assist into the air. Walleys are usually only done as single jumps and as part of a step sequence.

Split Jump - a split jump is when the skater jumps high into the air and stretches both legs out to each side and appears to touch their toes with their hands, and then lands on a back outside edge. It can be a spectacular jump, particularly when done in quick succession.

These jumps are evaluated by the judges based on the quality of the edges on take-off, landing, and the air position, jump height, and number of rotations. See Chapter 6 on IJS scoring to learn more.

Why do skaters jump in the corners?

You may notice that many of the jumps are performed on the outer edges of the skating area, and rarely in the middle. This is partly due to skating mechanics, and the need to build up sufficient speed going into the jump. But it is also due to common "skate etiquette" during practice sessions. Skaters generally are taught to keep jumps out of the middle of the ice. The middle of the ice is usually designated as the "spinning" area in practice sessions. This is a safety issue, as it is difficult for skaters in a spin to avoid someone going into or coming out of a jump.

Chapter 5

The Competitive Performance

This section will describe the differences between the competition requirements for each of the four different skating disciplines.

Singles Freestyle Skating

Singles freestyle skating is usually the first thing people picture when thinking about figure skating. A lone skater on the ice, performing jumps, spins, and footwork with grace, artistry and style, along with power, speed and agility. Indeed it is the most popular and competitive form of figure skating.

The Short Program

The Short Program is the first competitive performance in the figure skating event. In the Short program, skaters have a required set of elements to perform, and a limited time for their music. The music can be no longer than 2:50 for both the mens and the ladies events. The required elements (as of 2017-2018 season) for the Short program are:

Senior Ladies (2:50 max)	Senior Men (2:50 max)
Double or Triple Axel	Double or Triple Axel
Any Triple Jump Immediately preceded by connecting steps or other free skating movements. May not repeat Triple Axel	Any Triple or Quadruple Jump Immediately preceded by connecting steps or other free skating movements. May not repeat Triple Axel
Jump Combination (Double/Triple or Triple/Triple. May not repeat Axel jump performed or solo jump)	Jump Combination (Double/Triple, Triple/Triple, Quad/Double, or Quad/Triple. May not repeat Axel jump performed or solo jump)
Flying Spin Landing position different than layback/sideways leaning spin Min. 8 revs	Flying Spin Landing position different than spin in 1 position Min. 8 revs.
Layback or Sideways Leaning Spin No flying entry Min. 8 revs.	Camel or Sit Spin With only 1 change of foot No flying entry Min. 6 revs. each foot
Spin Combination With only 1 change of foot No flying entry Min. 6 revs. each foot Min. 2 revs. in pos.	Spin Combination With only 1 change of foot No flying entry Min. 6 revs. each foot Min. 2 revs. in pos.
Leveled Step Sequence Fully utilizing the ice surface	Leveled Step Sequence Fully utilizing the ice surface

It is very important that all the required elements are met during the Short program performance. Missing a required element will result in mandatory deduction. Each competitor is given a set of scores based on The International Judging System, which will be further explained in Chapter 6.

To determine the "draw" or the order of skating for this first event at US Senior Nationals, the competitors are split in two groups based on their previous competitions. The skaters with automatic invitations draw at random for spots in the last two warm-up groups. The remaining skaters draw at random for the remaining spots. For events other than the Senior level, all spots are drawn at random for the first event.

The Free Skate

The Free Skate ("long") program is usually performed 1-2 days later. The time requirement for the Free skate is almost twice the length of the Short program. The starting order for this segment of the event is based on the finishing order from the Short program. The skaters are split into groups of 5 or 6 and draw randomly for the start order within that group. The top skaters from the Short program skate in the last group for the free program.

Free Skate Requirements

Senior Ladies (4:00 +/- 10 sec)	Senior Men (4:30 +/- 10 sec)
Maximum of 7 jump elements: • One must be an Axel-type jump • Max. 3 jump combinations (combos) or sequences • Combos limited to 2 jumps, but one 3-jump combo is permitted • Number of jumps in jump sequence is not limited • 2 triples or quads may be repeated, but must be in combo or sequence • Max. 2 double Axels as solo jump or in combo/sequence	**Maximum of 8 jump elements:** • One must be an Axel-type jump • Max. 3 jump combinations (combos) or sequences • Combos limited to 2 jumps, but one 3-jump combo is permitted • Number of jumps in jump sequence is not limited • 2 triples or quads may be repeated, but must be in combo or sequence • Max. 2 double Axels as solo jump or in combo/sequence

Maximum of 3 spins:	Maximum of 3 spins:
<ul><li>1 flying entry</li><li>1 spin combination; with or without change of foot</li><li>1 spin with only 1 position</li><li>Min. 6 revolutions; 10 revolutions for combo</li><li>Min. 2 revolutions in position</li><li>All spins may change feet and start with a fly</li><li>Spins must be of a different nature</li></ul>	<ul><li>1 flying entry</li><li>1 spin combination; with or without change of foot</li><li>1 spin with only 1 position</li><li>Min. 6 revolutions; 10 revolutions for combo</li><li>Min. 2 revolutions in position</li><li>All spins may change feet and start with a fly</li><li>Spins must be of a different nature</li></ul>
One leveled step sequence* One choreographic sequence Fully utilizing the ice surface	One leveled step sequence* One choreographic sequence Fully utilizing the ice surface

The scores from the Short Program and the Free Skate are combined, and the top four skaters are awarded medals: Gold, Silver, Bronze and Pewter. The first-place winner is given the title of "{year} US National Champion", and can use that title for the rest of his or her career. A more detailed explanation of the scoring is found in Chapter 6, The IJS.

*A "leveled" step sequence refers to the Difficulty Level as determined by the International Judging System. More information on this can be found in Chapter 6.

Pairs Skating

Pairs is perhaps the most exciting of the figure skating disciplines. During a twist lift, the female skater may be 9 feet or more off the ice, with only her partner between her and catastrophe. The spins and lifts done by pairs skaters can be spectacular.

Because there are fewer competitors than in the singles discipline, pairs skaters start their competition year at the Sectional event. The top four teams in each section advance to the National Championship. Those assigned a

Death spiral. Photo credit: Kevin Rushforth CC BY-SA 3.0

"bye" or automatic invitation as described for the Singles competitors also compete at the national event.

At US Nationals the Senior competitors are split in two groups based on their previous competitions. The skaters with automatic invitations draw at random for spots in the last two warm-up groups. The remaining skaters draw at random for the remaining spots.

Senior Pairs Short Program Requirements. Music 2:40 +/- 10 sec

Lifts	Twist Lift	Throw Jump	Solo Jump	Pair Spin/ Combination	Death Spiral	Leveled Step Sequence
Any hip lift take off	Double or Triple	Double or Triple Flip or Lutz	Double or Triple, any jump	One change of foot, min 8 revolutions	Forward Inside	Full utilization of the ice

Senior Pairs Free Skate Program Requirements: Music 4:30 +/- 10 sec

Lifts	Twist Lift	Throw Jump	Solo Jump	Jump Sequence / Combination	Solo Spin/ Combination	Pair Spin/ Combination	Death Spiral	Choreo- graphed Sequence
Max 3 Overhead Lifts	Max 1 Twist Lift	Max 2 Throw Jumps	Max 1 Side by side Jump	Max 1	Max 1 Min 10 revolutions	Max 1 Min 8 revolutions	Max 1 Must be different than Short program	Clearly recognizable

As in the Singles events, the scores from the Short Program and the Free Skate are combined, and the top four pairs teams are awarded medals: Gold, Silver, Bronze and Pewter. The first-place winner is given the title of "{year} US National Champion" and can use that title for the rest of his or her career. A more detailed explanation of the scoring is found in Chapter 6, The IJS.

Ice Dancing

Ice dance is likely the oldest form of figure skating. Ice skaters in the Victorian era would try to recreate on ice the waltzes and other dances that were popular at the time. Over time, those patterns became the foundation of the ice dance discipline. Currently there are 33 dance patterns of waltzes, tangos, rhumbas, marches, and cha-chas.

Although ice dance is quite old, and figure skating first appeared in the winter games in 1908, it was not an event in the Olympics until 1972.

However, ice dance has undergone many changes over the 20 years. They were the first discipline allowed to use voice music in their programs, beginning in late 1990s. Then, in 2010 the structure of the event was changed dramatically. In the past, ice dance teams were required to skate a compulsory pattern dance, an original dance, and a Free Dance. Starting with the 2010-2011 season, the pattern dance requirement was eliminated, to make the event coincide more with the singles and pairs events. The original dance became the Short Dance, in which a compulsory pattern is a required part of the routine, but the rest of the routine is made up of original choreography. The Free Dance is the long program in ice dance, with requirements for footwork, lifts, spins and music.

There are 7 levels each of pattern dance tests, plus 5 moves in the field and Free Dance tests (Juvenile through Senior) that ice dance teams must pass to reach the senior competitive level.

Pattern Dance Tests

Test Level	Dances
Preliminary	Dutch Waltz, Canasta Tango, Rhythm Blues
Pre-Bronze	Swing Dance, Cha Cha, Fiesta Tango
Bronze	Hickory Hoedown, Willow Waltz, Ten-Fox
Pre-Silver	Fourteenstep, European Waltz, Foxtrot
Silver	American Waltz, Tango, Rocker Foxtrot
Pre-Gold	Killian, Blues, Paso Doble, Starlight Waltz
Gold	Viennese Waltz, Westminster Waltz, Quickstep, Argentine Tango

At US Nationals the Senior competitors are split in two groups based on their previous competitions. The skaters with automatic invitations draw at random for spots in the last two warm-up groups. The remaining skaters draw at random for the remaining spots. For events other than the Senior level, all spots are drawn at random for the first event.

Senior Ice Dance Short Program Requirements. Music 2:50 +/- 10 sec

Lifts	Step Sequences	Twizzles	Pattern Dance Element	Additional Information
1 Short Life, max 7 secs	1 Not Touching Sequence and 1 Pattern Dance Type Step Sequence	1 Set of Sequential Twizzles	One section of Rhumba dance pattern	Music Requirements: Latin America Rhythms, Cha Cha, Rhumba, Samba, Mambo, or any other closely related Latin American Rhythms

It is very important that all the required elements are met during the Short Dance performance. Missing a required element will result in mandatory deduction. Each competitor is given a set of scores based on The International Judging System, which will be further explained in Chapter 6.

The Free Dance

The Free Dance program is usually performed 1-2 days later. The time requirement for the Free Dance is almost twice as long as the Short Dance. The starting order is based on the finishing order from the Short Dance. The dance pairs are split into groups of 5 or 6 and draw randomly for the start order within that group. The top dance pairs from the Short Dance skate in the last group for the Free Dance.

Senior Ice Dance Free Dance Requirements. Music 4:00 +/- 10 sec

Lifts	Dance Spins	Step Sequences	Twizzles	Choreographic Element	Additional Information
Max 3 One short life (max 7 secs) and one combination lift.(max 12 sec) OR Three different short lifts	Max 1 Spin or Combination Spin - min 3 rev by both partners	Max 2	Max 1	2 Different 1 Choreographic Dance Lift OR 1 Choreographic Spinning OR 1 Choreographic Twizzling Movement	Violations: Separations for longer than 5 secs, unless at the beginning or end of the program which may be 10 sec During program stops up to 5 sec are permitted No touching the ice with hands, lying, kneeling or sitting. Jumps of more than one revolution or one revolution jumps in unison Illegal Lift, Movement or Pose

As in the Singles and Pairs events, the scores from the Short Dance and the Free Dance are combined, and the top four ice dance teams are awarded medals: Gold, Silver, Bronze and Pewter. The first place team is given the title of "{year} US National Champion", and can use that title for the rest of their careers. A more detailed explanation of the scoring is found in Chapter 6, The IJS.

Chapter 6
The International Judging System (IJS)

History of the change from 6.0 to IJS

If you are older than 18 you probably remember the "old" way of scoring figure skating - the 6.0 system. In this system, which is still used in a few of the lower figure skating levels, an odd numbered panel of judges (3, 5, 7 or 9) give marks on technical merit and presentation, ranging from 0 to 6.0. The best score was 6.0, and the audience knew when a 6.0 flashed on the scoreboard, they had witnessed something special. So why did it have to change?

The problem with the 6.0 system is that it was highly subjective. The scores were based solely on the judge's perception of the performance. There were rules for mandatory deductions for falls and missed jumps, but the scoring could be highly influenced on other factors than the actual skating.

At the 2002 Winter Olympic games in Salt Lake City, a French judge and a Russian judge were suspected of "score swapping". The French judge agreed to mark the leading pairs team from Canada down so the Russian team would win, and the Russian judge would help with scores for the French ice dance team the next day. However, the Canadian team skated such an obviously better long program than the Russian team that it was suspected that the French judge was being purposely unfair. When confronted by the ISU officials, the French judge admitted to the scandal. She was suspended for three years from figure skating and the Canadian team was awarded co-gold medals with the Russian team.

Clearly changes needed to be made to the scoring system to make it less subjective. A new system was developed over the course of two years and implemented starting in late 2003. The International Judging System, or IJS, uses a much more defined and technical system for awarding points. There are still areas for subjective scores, but the system makes it difficult for any one judge to "throw" a competition.

How does the scoring system work?

The IJS uses two scoring elements for each skater's performance, the Total Element Score (TES) and the Program Component Score (PCS). The TES score is based on the technical execution of the jumps, spins, and step sequences. The PCS score is based on the program's choreography, style, musicality, and other stylistic factors of the performance. The TES and the PCS are combined to create a Total Segment Score (TSS) for each segment of the event (one for the Short Program or Short Dance, one for the Free Skate or Free Dance). The TSS for each segment are combined for the Total Competition Score (TCS). The competition final ranking is determined by the Total Competition Score at the end of the event.

IJS Officials

In the IJS system, the task of awarding points to each skater is divided among several judges, each with their own task. There is a **Technical Panel** of 5 technical skating experts that review each element and makes the "call" whether the element met the technical requirements. The **Judging Panel**, comprised of a referee and 3-9 judges (9 at Championship events), are responsible for scoring the quality of the element performed, and over skating skills, captured in the Program Component Score.

The Technical Element Score (TES)

Technical Element Scores for Jumps

Each of the elements, jumps, spins and step sequences, are assigned difficulty ratings. These ratings are reviewed every year by the ISU, and the tables are published on the ISU website. The 2017/2018 Scale of Values can be found on www.isu.org, ISU Communication 2089. {http://www.isu.org/communications/14352-isu-communication-2089/file}

The order of difficulty and base values in the IJS for the 2017-2018 season are as follows:

Singles and Pairs Solo Jump Base values in IJS

Jump	Single (1)	Double (2)	Triple (3)	Quad (4)
Toe loop (T)	0.4	1.3	4.3	10.3
Salchow (S)	0.4	1.3	4.4	10.5
Loop (Lo)	0.5	1.8	5.1	12.0
Flip (F)	0.5	1.9	5.3	12.3
Lutz (Lz)	0.6	2.1	6.0	13.6
Axel (A)	1.1	3.3	8.5	15.0

As you can see, double, triple, and quadruple rotation jumps increase the base value of difficulty. Jumps that are done in the second half of the program are given additional 10% credit since it is more difficult to execute jumps well when tired.

Jumps are referred to in the judging sheets by the rotation number and letter. A double axel is 2A, a quad flip is 4F, and double loop - double toe loop combination is 2Lo+2T.

A fall on a jump requires a -1 off the Total Segment Score.

Each judge also gives a Grade of Execution (GOE) score for each technical element performed. The GOE given corresponds to a addition or reduction in points to the base value. See Chapter 7 on Grade of Execution scores for more details.

Technical Element Scores for Spins

Spins also have a hierarchy of difficulty and scoring. Generally, the skills of the spins involve the number of rotations, change of foot, flying or unusual entrance, and changes in position. Spins are assigned "Levels of Difficulty", called Basic, 1, 2, 3, and 4. The Levels of Difficulty listed in ISU Communication 2089 are as follows:

Number of features for Levels: 1 for Level 1, 2 for Level 2, 3 for Level 3, 4 for Level 4

1. Difficult variations (count as many times as performed with limitations specified below)
2. Change of foot executed by jump
3. Jump within a spin without changing feet
4. Difficult change of position on the same foot
5. Difficult entrance into a spin
6. Clear change of edge in sit (only from backward inside to forward outside), camel, Layback and Biellmann position
7. All 3 basic positions on the second foot
8. Both directions immediately following each other in sit or camel spin
9. Clear increase of speed in camel, sit, layback or Biellmann position
10. At least 8 rev. without changes in position/variation, foot or edge (camel, layback, difficult variation of any basic position or for combinations only non-basic position)
11. Difficult variation of flying entry in flying spins/spins with a flying entrance (see Clarifications)

Additional features for the Layback spin:

12. One clear change of position backwards-sideways or reverse, at least 2 rev. in each position (counts also if the Layback spin is a part of any other spin)
13. Biellmann position after Layback spin (SP – after 8 revolutions in layback spin)

Feature 2-9, 11-13 count only once per program (first time they are attempted). Feature 10 counts only once per program (in the first spin it is successfully performed; if in this spin 8 revs are executed on both feet, any one of these executions can be taken in favor of the skater).

Any category of difficult spin variation in a basic position counts only once per program (first time it is attempted). A difficult variation in a non-basic position counts once per program in spin combination only (first time it is attempted).

In any spin with change of foot the maximum number of features attained on one foot is two (2)

As you can see, the skater is rewarded with extra credit for unusual spins, unusual entrance into the spin, gaining speed during the spin, spinning at least 8 revolutions per position, changing feet, changing positions, and spinning in a position that requires unusual strength and/or flexibility. Additional information and clarifications regarding the judging and leveling of spins can be found in ISU Communication 2089. Senior level competitors are expected to perform Level 4 spins.

Technical Element Scores for Step Sequences

Step sequences, or footwork steps, are also given Levels of Difficulty, based on the following from ISU Communication 2089: {http://www.isu.org/communications/14352-isu-communication-2089/file}

Number of features for Levels: 1 for Level 1, 2 for Level 2, 3 for Level 3, 4 for Level 4
1. *Minimum variety (Level 1), simple variety (Level 2), variety (Level 3), complexity (Level 4) of difficult turns and steps throughout (**compulsory**)*
2. *Rotations in either direction (left and right) with full body rotation covering at least 1/3 of the pattern in total for each rotational direction*
3. *Use of body movements for at least 1/3 of the pattern*
4. *Two different combinations of 3 difficult turns on different feet executed with a clear rhythm within the sequence. Only the **first combination** attempted on each foot can be counted.*

The skater is rewarded for variety in footwork, complexity and difficulty of turns, and usage of body movements and coverage of the ice arena. Additional information and clarifications regarding the judging and leveling of step sequences can be found in ISU Communication 2089. Senior level competitors are expected to perform Level 4 step sequences.

Technical Element Scores for Pairs Skating

Pairs skating elements are also assigned Levels of Difficulty. For the 2017/2018 season, the Levels of Difficulty, as given by the ISU Communication 2089, are as follows:

{http://www.isu.org/communications/14352-isu-communication-2089/file}

Twist Lifts	1. Lady's split position (each leg at least 45° from the body axis and Lady's legs are straight or almost straight) 2. Catching the lady at the side of the waist without her hand(s)/arm(s)/any part of upper body touching the man 3. Lady's position in the air with arm(s) above the head (minimum one full revolution) 4. Difficult take-off 5. Man's arms sideways, being straight or almost straight, reaching at least shoulder level after release of the lady
Lifts	1. Seniors: Difficult variation of the take-off and/or difficult landing variety Juniors: Simple variation of the take-off and/or simple landing variety (each counts as a feature) 2. 1 change of hold and/or lady's position (1 rev. of the man before and after the change, counts twice if repeated) 3. Difficult variation of the lady (one full revolution) 4. Difficult (simple for juniors) carry (not for SP) 5. One-hand-hold of the man (2 full revolutions in total not counting parts shorter than 1 rev.) 6. Additional revolutions of the man with one-hand-hold after 2 revs in 5 (only in Free Skate and only in one lift) 7. Change of rotational direction by the man (one rev. before and after the change, counts only once per program) Features 1), 2), 3) must be *significantly* different from lift to lift and if similar, will only count first time attempted.

Step Sequence	1. Minimum variety (Level 1), simple variety (Level 2), variety (Levels 3–4) of difficult turns and steps of both partners throughout (compulsory)
2. Rotations in either direction (left and right) with full body rotation covering at least 1/3 of the pattern in total for each rotational direction)
3. Use of body movements for at least 1/3 of the pattern
4. Changes of position (crossing at least three times while doing steps and turns) for at least 1/3 of the sequence, but not more than 1/2 of the sequence or not separating at least half of the pattern (changes of holds are allowed)
5. Two different combinations of 3 difficult turns (rockers, counters, brackets, twizzles, loops) executed by both partners with a clear rhythm within the sequence
Death Spirals	1. *Difficult entry (immediately preceding the death spiral) and/or exit*
2. *Full revolution(s) of the lady when both partners are in "low" positions (counts as many times as performed)*
Solo Spins	1. *Difficult variations (count as many times as performed with limitations specified below)*
2. *Change of foot executed by jump*
3. *Jump within a spin without changing feet*
4. *Difficult change of position on the same foot*
5. *Difficult entrance into a spin*
6. *Clear change of edge in sit (only from backward inside to forward outside), camel, Layback and Biellmann Position*
7. *All 3 basic positions on the second foot*
8. *Both directions immediately following each other in sit or camel spin*
9. *Clear increase of speed in camel, sit, layback or Biellmann position*
10. *At least 6 rev. without changes in position/variation, foot and edge (camel, layback, difficult variation of any basic position or for combinations only non-basic position)*

Features 2 to 10 and any category of difficult spin variation count only once per program (first time attempted). If 6 revs are executed on both feet, any one of these executions can be taken in favor of the skaters. In any spin with change of foot the maximum number of features attained on one foot is two (2). |

Pairs Spins	1. 3 changes of basic positions of both partners 2. 3 difficult variations of positions of partners, only one of which can be in non-basic position (each variation of each partner counts separately, each partner must have at least one difficult variation) 3. Any other difficult variation in a basic position of either partner (each partner must have two difficult variations) 4. Entrance from backward outside or inside edge 5. Both directions immediately following each other 6. At least 6 revolutions without any changes in position/variation and foot (camel, sit, difficult upright)

Technical Element Scores for Ice Dance

Levels of Difficulty for Ice Dance for the 2017/2018 season are given in ISU Communication 2086
{http://www.isu.org/communications/581-isu-communication-2086/file}

Levels of Difficulty for Spins

Level 1	Level 2	Level 3	Level 4
Spin: at least 3 rotations **Combination Spin**: at least 3 rotations in either part and more than 1 rotation on other part	**OPTION 1** 2 different Difficult Variations from 2 different Basic Positions **OPTION 2** 1 Difficult Variation from any Basic Position	**OPTION 1** 3 different Difficult Variations from 3 different Basic Positions **OPTION 2** 2 different Difficult Variations from 2 different Basic Positions	**OPTION 1** 4 different Difficult Variations from 3 different Basic Positions (at least 2 different Difficult Variations being performed by partners simultaneously). AND Entry feature or Exit feature **OPTION 2** 3 different Difficult Variations from 3 different Basic Positions AND Entry feature or Exit feature

Additional information including extensive information on the Levels of Difficulty for Dance Lifts can be found in ISU Communication 2086 {http://www.isu.org/communications/581-isu-communication-2086/file}

Chapter 7
Grades of Execution (GOE)

Judges award the skater a Grade of Execution (GOE) for each program element performed. GOE scores range from -3 to +3, including 0. Each GOE mark corresponds to a point addition or deduction that is combined with the Base Value. This scoring chart is given in ISU Communication 2089.

{http://www.isu.org/communications/14352-isu-communication-2089/file}.

An example of the GOE point additions or deductions for a double axel is given below:

Jump	+3	+2	+1	Base	V	-1	-2	-3
Double Axel (2A)	1.5	1.0	0.5	3.3	2.3	-0.5	-1.0	-1.5

If a jump is slightly under-rotated, that is, the skater lands 1/4 to 1/2 turn too early, the jump is marked with a < on the scoring chart, and a different base value is used, indicated by the **V** column above.

Criteria for positive GOEs in jumps

Positive GOEs are given based on the skaters based on the quality jump, creative entry originality and creativity, and/or good height and distance. There are extensive rules for judges to follow in giving positive GOE scores. The list of criteria for jumps are given below and can be found in ISU Communication 2089:

31

{http://www.isu.org/communications/14352-isu-communication-2089/file}

Judges award positive GOEs in jumps for the reasons shown below. Multiple items achieved in the same element increase the GOE score.

For +1 GOE : 2 bullets
For +2 GOE : 4 bullets
For +3 GOE : 6 or more bullets

Criteria for Positive GOEs in Jumps
- unexpected / creative / difficult entry
- clear recognizable (creative, interesting, original for jump preceded by steps/movements of the Short Program) steps/free skating movements immediately preceding element
- varied position in the air / delay in rotation
- good height and distance
- good extension on landing / creative exit
- good flow from entry to exit including jump combinations / sequences
- effortless throughout
- element matched to the musical structure

Criteria for Negative GOEs for Jumps

For jumps there are many reasons for the judges to give negative GOEs, including a fall, having less than the required number of rotations, second jump not performed in a combination jump, landing on two feet, stepping out of the landing of the jump, touching down with one or both hands, questionable edge take off on flip or lutz, and poor speed, height, distance and/or air position of the jump.

The chart below shows examples of what the judge's final GOE score must take into account. For example, if the jump was executed very well but there was a fall on the landing, the judge will consider the score he/she would have given, reduce by the mandatory amount, and give the final score. In this case, the judge may have awarded a +2 for the jump, but subtract 3 for the fall, for a final GOE score of -1 for the element. A fall also requires -1.00 points from the overall Total Segment Score. More criteria may be found in ISU Communication 2089.

Criteria for Negative GOE in Jumps	GOE Reduced by
In the Short program, one or more revolutions less than required for a jump	-3
In the Short program, combination jump consisting of only one jump, Final GOE must be -3.	-3
Downgrade sign <<	-3
In the Short program, no required steps or movements preceding the jump	-3
Fall	-3
Landing on two feet in a jump	-3
Stepping out of the landing in a jump	-3
Touch down with both hands in a jump	-2
2 three turns in between jumps in a combination jump	-2
Starting on the wrong edge in a flip or lutz	-2 to -3
Poor height, speed, distance and/or air position in a jump	-1 to -2
Lacking rotation (no sign from technical panel)	-1
Under-rotated (with < sign from technical panel)	-1 to -2
In the Short program, a break between the required steps/movements and the jump, or only one step or movement	-1 to -2
Poor positions	-1 to -3
Loss of flow/rhythm between jumps in a combination or sequence jump	-1 to -2
Weak landing, including wrong edge, scratching, or bad position	-1 to -2
Long preparation (telegraphing)	-1 to -2
Touch down with one hand or free foot	-1
Unclear edge at take-off in Flip or Lutz, (sign "e" from technical panel)	-1 to -2

Criteria for positive GOEs in spins

Positive GOEs are given based on the skaters based on the quality of the spin in speed, center, balance, number of rotations, creativity and matched to the music. There are extensive rules for judges to follow in giving positive GOE scores. The list of criteria for spins are given below and more can be found in ISU Communication 2089.

For +1 GOE : 2 bullets
For +2 GOE : 4 bullets
For +3 GOE : 6 or more bullets

Reasons for Positive GOEs in Spins
• *good speed or acceleration during spin*
• *ability to center a spin quickly*
• *balanced rotations in all positions*
• *clearly more than required number of revolutions*
• *good, strong position(s) (including height and air/landing position in flying spins)*
• *creativity and originality*
• *good control throughout all phases*
• *element matched to the musical structure*

Criteria for Negative GOEs in Spins

There are also mandatory -1 to -3 GOE reductions for having less than the required number of rotations in a spin, not achieving the correct position in spin, having one or two hands touch down, traveling, slow speed, and general poor execution. As in the above example with jumps, these are reductions, not final GOE scores. If the spin was excellent and worth a +3, but the spin traveled slightly (the skater drifted while spinning) the overall GOE would be +2. More criteria may be found in ISU Communication 2089.

Criteria for Negative GOEs in Spins	GOE Reduced by
Fall	-3
Less than the required revolutions	-1 to -2
Less than the required number of positions or revolutions in position	-2 to -3
Touching down with both hands	-2
Poor or awkward position, slow, and/or traveling spin	-1 to -3
Poor air position in a flying spin	-1 to -3
Change of foot during spin poorly executed	-1 to -3
Incorrect take-off or landing in a flying spin	-1 to -2
Touching down with one hand or with free foot	-1
Traveling	-1 to -3
Unbalanced number of revolutions in change foot spin	-1

Chapter 8
Program Component Score

Along with the Technical Score Elements (TES), the judges give a Program Components Score (PCS). The Program Components Score is the way the judges award the more objective and stylistic part of figure skating. This score is given for the entire performance, not per element. The skills judged in the Program Component Score are: (from the US Figure Skating website) {http://www.usfsa.org/story?id=84064}

The 5 Categories for the Program Component Score

Skill	Description
Skating Skills	Use of deep edges, steps and turns
	Balance, rhythmic knee action and precision of foot placement
	Flow and glide
	Varied use of power, speed and acceleration
	Use of multi directional skating
	Use of one-foot skating

Transitions/Linking Footwork and Movements	*Continuity of movements from one element to another*
	Variety (including variety of holds in ice dancing)
	Difficulty
	Quality
Performance and Execution	*Physical, emotional and intellectual involvement and projection*
	Carriage and clarity of movement
	Variety and contrast of movements and energy
	Individuality / personality
	Unison and "oneness"
	Spatial awareness between partners – management of the distance between skaters and management of changes of hold (pairs skating, ice dancing)
Choreography and Composition	*Purpose (idea, concept, vision, mood);*
	Pattern / ice coverage;
	Multidimensional use of space and design of movements;
	Phrase and form (movements and parts structured to match the musical phrase);
	Originality of the composition.

Interpretation	*Movement and steps in time to the music (timing)* *Expression of the music's character/feeling and rhythm, when clearly identifiable* *Use of finesse to reflect the details and nuances of the music (Finesse is the skaters' refined, artful manipulation of music details and nuances through movement. It is unique to the skater/skaters and demonstrates an inner feeling for the music and the composition. Nuances are the personal ways of bringing subtle variations to the intensity, tempo and dynamics of the music made by the composer and/or musicians.)* *Relationship between the skaters reflecting the character and rhythm of the music (pair skating, ice dancing);* *Skating primarily to the rhythmic beat for short dance and keeping a good balance between skating to the beat and melody in the free dance (ice dancing)*

PCS Scores are marked on a scale of 0.25 to 10, in increments of 0.25. There are separate marks given for each component listed above.

0.25-0.75 = Extremely poor
1.00-1.75 = Very poor
2.00-2.75 = Poor
3.00-3.75 = Weak
4.00-4.75 = Fair
5.00-5.75 = Average
6.00-6.75 = Above average
7.00-7.75 = Good
8.00-8.75 = Very good
9.00-9.75 = Superior
10.00 = Outstanding

The Program Component Score is calculated and factored by a specified percentage for each segment (that is, the short program and long program) of each event. The factoring allows the PCS to have roughly equal weight with the Technical Elements Score when combined for the Total Segment Score.

Chapter 9
Total Competition Score

Finally, the performances are over. The final score, the Total Competition Score, is awarded to each skater. To review, each skated performance receives a Technical Elements Score (TES) and a Program Components Score (PCS), and any mandatory deductions for falls or program violations. These are combined and the performance is awarded a Total Segment Score (TSS). At the end of the competition the Total Segment Scores for each performance (Short Program and Free Program) are combined to reach a Total Competition Score, and placements are awarded based on this score.

What score do you need to win a competition?

While watching a skating event, you may wonder what "good scores" are for each event. Below is a sample of the range of scores in the 2018 US National Championships for each discipline.

Senior Ladies

Placement	Short Program (TES + PCS - Deduction = TSS)	Free Skate (TES + PCS - Deduction = TSS)	Total Competition Score
1	40.88 + 32.91 - 0 = 73.79	76.01 + 69.71 - 0 = 145.72	219.51
2	41.90 + 31.19 - 0 = 73.09	73.33 + 67.42 - 0 = 140.75	213.84
3	35.68 + 33.80 - 0 = 69.48	62.25 + 68.00 - 0 = 130.25	199.73
10	33.52 + 26.77 - 0 = 60.29	52.70 + 48.87 - 0 = 101.57	161.86
Last	20.09 + 21.81 - 1 = 40.90	22.05 + 39.59 - 2 = 59.64	100.54

Senior Men

Placement	Short Program (TES + PCS - Deduction = TSS)	Free Skate (TES + PCS - Deduction = TSS)	Total Competition Score
1	57.91 + 46.54 - 0 = 104.45	76.01 + 69.71 - 0 = 145.72	250.17
2	49.62 + 46.90 - 0 = 96.52	73.33 + 67.42 - 0 = 140.75	237.27
3	45.94 + 47.29 - 0 = 93.23	62.25 + 68.00 - 0 = 130.25	223.48
10	40.60 + 39.00 - 0 = 79.60	52.70 + 48.87 - 0 = 101.57	181.17
Last	23.51 + 29.50 - 1 = 52.04	47.81 + 45.66 -1 = 92.47	144.51

Senior Pairs

Placement	Short Program (TES + PCS - Deduction = TSS)	Free Skate (TES + PCS - Deduction = TSS)	Total Competition Score
1	37.99 + 33.11 - 0 = 71.10	66.50 + 70.00 - 1 = 135.50	206.6
2	37.58 + 31.35 - 0 = 68.93	65.23 + 67.64 - 1 = 131.87	200.8
3	37.33 + 30.51 - 0 = 67.84	67.61 + 63.20 - 1 = 129.81	197.65
10	27.86 + 23.29 - 0 = 51.15	53.46 + 49.64 - 0 = 103.10	154.25
Last	24.12 + 18.85 - 2 = 40.97	43.90 + 42.45 - 2 = 84.35	125.32

Senior Dance

Placement	Short Dance (TES + PCS - Deduction = TSS)	Free Dance (TES + PCS - Deduction = TSS)	Total Competition Score
1	43.64 + 38.69 - 0 = 82.33	61.39 + 57.60 - 0 = 118.99	201.32
2	40.96 + 38.14 - 0 = 79.10	59.77 + 58.25 - 0 = 118.02	197.12
3	39.95 + 37.66 - 0 = 77.61	57.26 + 57.34 - 0 = 114.60	192.21
10	29.37 + 25.16 - 0 = 54.53	44.01 + 37.83 - 0 = 81.84	136.37
Last	17.77 + 14.40 - 1 = 31.17	28.89 + 20.36 - 1 = 48.25	79.42

Chapter 10
Figure Skating Judges

The judges box has become a bit crowded with the adoption of the IJS. The entire judging team consists of the 5-person Technical Panel, and a 3-9 person Judging Panel, and the Referee. Each person in the judges box has a particular duty to fulfill during the performance.

The Technical Panel

The **technical specialist** is the judge responsible for identifying the elements the skater performs, and for making "the call" on the correctness of the element. If a jump is under-rotated, a fall occurs, an incorrect edge is used, there are not enough revolutions in spins, or any other fault in a planned element, the technical specialist informs the rest of the judges.

The **assistant technical specialist** acts as a "backup" to the technical specialist. This judge may call for a review if he or she is not in agreement or is not sure of the call of the technical specialist. The **technical controller** is the leader of the technical panel. The technical call for an element is decided by the majority rule of these three judges. The audio of their judgments is recorded and available for review after the performance.

To assist in the decision making the technical specialists and technical controller may review the video captured by the **video replay operator**. The video replay operator can instantly bring the video of an element back for review, so the technical specialists can make the right call.

Once the call is made, the **data operator** enters the coding on paper or into the computer so that the judging panel may give Grade of Execution scores on the elements, including any mandatory deductions.

The Judging Panel

The role of the **judges** on the Judging Panel is to focus on the quality of each element performed, to award the Grade of Execution (GOE) Score, and to give an overall performance score for each of the 5 criteria in the Program Component Score (PCS). After each element is performed, the judge reviews the information provided by the technical panel and awards the GOE score, keeping in mind any necessary deductions for faults in the execution of the element as decided by the technical panel.

The **referee** is the leader of the judging panel. The job of the referee is to ensure that the rules are being followed, to be the contact person to the skater if there is a problem with her music or equipment, to keep track of program times, and decide on any protests that may be filed during or after the event.

A Guided Tour Through Judging a Competition

Let's put it all together and take a look behind-the-scenes at the judge's box at an IJS figure skating competition using a hypothetical skating performance.

A Senior Ladies competitor enters the ice to perform her short program. As she takes her starting pose on the ice, the **referee** prepares to time her. The time clock does not start until the skater makes her first move, which may be immediately or several seconds after the music starts. The referee will continue to time until she stops movement at the end of her performance. If the skater is not within the required time for the event, the referee will inform the rest of the technical panel and a mandatory point deduction will be made.

Several weeks prior to the competition, she and her coach submitted a Planned Program Content (PPC) to the governing body of the competition. The PPC gives the official abbreviation of each element, the order of the elements, and the approximate time the element will be attempted in the program. This PPC will be the guide, also called the "judging protocol", used to judge the skater's performance.

As she prepares for her first element, usually a jump, the **technical specialist, assistant technical specialist and technical controller** are watching her feet, primarily, to establish that the jump takeoff was on the proper edge, the jump had the required number of rotations, and the landing edge was solid and correct. They will be looking for under-rotated jumps (even ¼ turn short will earn a deduction in GOE), a two-foot landing (even a slight toe pick from the free foot with earn a deduction), and any touch down with the hand or free foot. If the panel is satisfied the jump was correct, they will mark it as "green". If there is a question about an element they may mark it as "yellow" for review. When it has been determined that an error occurred, the element is marked with "red". Notations may also be made on the judging protocol sheet. To go back to review an element, the technical specialists call on the **video replay operator** to quickly replay the element so a determination may be made. Once the decision has been made, the **data operator** enters it into the computer for the judges to award GOE scores.

While the technical panel is watching for technical issues, the **judges** on the judging panel are watching for overall quality. Did the jump have a great air position, speed, height, distance and flow in and out? Was there anything creatively unusual about the execution of the element? Did it look effortless, and did it match the mood and rhythm of the music? These are the aspect of the performance that are important to the judges awarding the GOE scores, and the overall PCS scores.

This process continues for each element in her performance. When she finishes her program, the members of the judging team make final evaluations, discuss any elements that are unclear, and enter the final scores. The computer then tallies the scores and the skater is awarded the Total Element Score and the Program Component Score, minus any deductions, to give a Total Segment Score for the performance.

For an extremely in-depth look at the Singles Event judging instructions for the IJS, consult the ISU Judging System Technical Panel Handbook, Single Skating at https://www.usfigureskating.org/content/Technical%20Panel%20Handbook_Singles%20Skating.pdf

(other disciplines are also available)

Chapter 11
The Winter Olympics

How are Olympic Skaters chosen?

Each country holds their qualifying competitions to determine who will be on the Olympic team. In the United States, the US Figure Skating National Championships are held about a month prior to the Olympics. At the conclusion of the Championships, the USFS committee makes a decision on who should be named to the team. The placement at nationals is important, but so is the placement in the previous year's World championships, the skaters' finishes at the Grand Prix events and the Grand Prix final in the autumn, and placement in other international competitions. The top medalists at nationals are not always the members of the Olympic team. For example, in the 2018 US Figure Skating Championships, the final top three in the men's event were Nathan Chen, Ross Miner and Vincent Zhou. The US had 3 spots for the men's event at the 2018 Winter Olympics. But Miner's placements in the previous events and the autumn international competitions were not as strong as the fourth-place finisher Adam Rippon. The committee voted to send Rippon instead of Miner. It was a controversial move with some skating fans. However, the committee believed that Rippon had a better chance to place well at the Olympic Games than Miner did.

Country qualifications for the Olympics

To earn competitor spots in the Winter Olympics Figure Skating Events:

Number of skaters/ teams entered at the previous World Championship (per discipline)	To Earn 3 Olympic Entries	To Earn 2 Olympic Entries	To Earn 1 Olympic Entry
1	Place in the top 2	Place in the top 10	Next best ranked athletes from countries not already assigned spots, until quota is filled.
2	Total of placements is equal to or less than 13	Total of placements is equal to or less than 28	
3	Sum of the top two placements is equal to or less than 13	Sum of the top two placements is equal to or less than 28	

Olympic Team Event

Established in the 2014 Olympics, the Team event in figure skating gives country teams a chance to compete as a team and country rather than only as individuals. This is similar to the team event in gymnastics. Each team selects representative in the four disciplines of figure skating to represent the team. The best combined team score wins.

Ten countries qualify to compete in the team event, based on the results of the international competitions in the prior year's World Figure Skating Championships, the ISU Grand Prix events, and other important skating competitions in the previous season. For the 2018 PyeongChang Winter Olympics, the qualifying teams are:

1. Canada
2. Russia* (or the Unified Team)
3. United States
4. Japan
5. China
6. Italy
7. France
8. Germany
9. Israel
10. South Korea

Alternate: Australia

Each team consists of a man, a woman, a pairs team and an ice dancing team. Two substitutions of single skaters or teams are allowed; for example, in the 2014 Olympic Games in Sochi, Russia, Ashley Wagner performed the ladies Short program and Gracie Gold performed the ladies Free Skate program. the men's events were split between Jeremy Abbott and Jason Brown.

The programs are scored using the standard International Judging System (IJS) as in the individual competitions. Points are awarded based on the finishing order of each event. The highest scoring skater or team is awarded 10 points, the 2nd place is awarded 9 points, 3rd place is awarded 8 points, and so on. After all the Short programs in each of the four skating disciplines are completed, the points are added for each team. The top five teams are allowed to move to the Free Skate/Free Dance events. The Free Skate/ Free Dance events are scored in the same way and medals are awarded to the top 3 teams. Then the individual events take place.

The addition of the new Team event is generally thought of as very positive. The skaters enjoy working for a team goal, and the extra time in front of the Olympic audience is a great warm up to the individual events that start a few days later.

Chapter 12
The Fun Stuff

Dresses and Costumes

Since 2006 ladies have been able to choose between wearing a dress or tights without an attached skirt. Men must wear trousers, not tight-fitting pants. Traditionally longer skirts are worn in ice dance programs to more resemble ballroom dancing. The costumes are often exquisitely decorated with rhinestones and beads; however, it is imperative that the decorations be very securely attached. Judges can take deductions for and excessive shedding of decorations from costumes. The women's dresses have evolved over the last 20 years to be more revealing. However, much of the time what may look like exposed skin is actually covered by skin-colored stretch material of spandex or mesh.

Music

Music is a huge part of the figure skating experience. The choice of which music to perform can make or break a figure skating routine. Rousing music selections can really get the audience on the side of the skater. Indeed, connection with the audience, interpretation and feeling of the music is part of the Program Component Score in the IJS system. Some skaters can really capture hearts with a lilting soft piano piece, where others will do their best skating to a classic rock jam. Either way it is important for the skater to find music that speaks to them personally and that they can interpret with their heart and soul.

In ice dance that style of music chosen is determined by the International Skating Union. In the 2017-2018 season including the Olympic games, ice dance teams are required to have music suitable for a rhumba dance, that is, Latin American music or similar. However, the teams are free to choose their own music, provided that it meets the strict requirements of tempo and style.

The 2018 Winter Games will be the first Olympics that all skaters have the choice of using vocal music for their performances. Skating music was once restricted to only instrumental music. Starting in 1997 for ice dancers and in 2014 for all skating disciplines, skating music may now include vocals.

Skates

Skating boots and blades have evolved over the last 10-15 years as well. Traditionally boots were made of stiff leather and blades were limited to maybe 4-5 different choices at the top levels. Now, new synthetic boots are available and are very popular with some skaters.

Blades choices have also grown tremendously. Different blade materials and construction such as parabolic and revolution blades, give the skater additional choices in their equipment. The new blades are advertised as being lighter, stronger and more flexible. The Revolution blades are easily recognizable with the support going to the middle of the blade from the boot, unlike traditional blades that are open in that area. 2018 US National Champion and quad-master Nathan Chen uses Revolution blades.

Other competitive skating disciplines

Figures - Figure skating was named such because of the figures, based on variations of the Figure 8 pattern. This was a very large part of competitive figure skating. The scores on figures counted for 60% of the overall score, until 1968 when it was reduced to 50%. Over the next 20 years the compulsory figures became less and less weighed in the overall score. By 1990 the International Skating Union (ISU) voted to remove figures completely from the international competitions. In 1997 the United States Figure Skating Association also removed figures from the main competition requirements.

While figures are no longer required there are still some skaters, particularly adult skaters, who enjoy the quiet discipline and fine edges of the figure 8. The Ice Skating Institute, another skating body in the US, still hold regular national and international figures competitions.

Synchronized Skating - "Synchro" skating was first recognized as a competitive discipline in early 1980s. In synchro, a team of 12-20 skaters perform wheel, lines, blocks, and intersections choreographed to music. The performance is judged on precision, movements in unison, difficulty of elements, and general skating ability. The International Judging system is used in synchro competitions. There are national championships in Synchronized Skating as well as international competitions.

Solo Ice Dance - solo ice dance is very much what it sounds like. Skaters test and perform pattern dances and free dances solo, without a partner. They are judged on the same criteria as dance pairs as far as depth and correctness of edges, steps, speed and quietness of the blade.

Theater on Ice - Theater on Ice provides a way for skating teams to give a theatrical performance on ice as a group. There are several yearly competitions in the US, including a National Theater on Ice competition in June. Teams of 8-30 skaters tell a story, much as you would find at the theater or ballet.

Showcase - Showcase lets individuals give a theatrical performance through the use of music, props and skating elements to tell a story. The categories are light entertainment (humor or light-hearted fun), dramatic (pieces that express more serious or soulful topics) and interpretive, where skaters are given a piece of music only a few minutes before the event and are expected to interpret the music "on the fly". Showcase events are conducted by test level, however they are intended to be judged more on the interpretation of the music and connection with the audience than with difficulty of jumps and spins.

Resources

ISU Communication 2089-SINGLE & PAIR SKATING

Scale of Values, Levels of Difficulty and Guidelines for marking, Grade of Execution, season 2017/18

http://www.isu.org/communications/14352-isu-communication-2089/file

ISU Communication 2086 – ICE DANCE http://www.isu.org/communications/581-isu-communication-2086/file

US Figure Skating: www.usfsa.org

Photo Credits

Cover Photo: Young girl figure skater © Boris Ryaposov | Dreamstime.com EL

Page 10. Sit spin. By The original uploader was Vesperholly at English Wikipedia (Transferred from en.wikipedia to Commons.) [CC BY-SA 2.5 (https://creativecommons.org/licenses/by-sa/2.5)], via Wikimedia Commons.

Page 10. Pancake spin. By Luu (Own work) [CC BY-SA 3.0 (https://creativecommons.org/licenses/by-sa/3.0)], via Wikimedia Commons.

Page 10. Haircutter spin. By Doug Drew (Own work) [CC BY 3.0 (http://creativecommons.org/licenses/by/3.0)], via Wikimedia Commons.

Page 11. Biellmann spin. By David W. Carmichael (http://davecskatingphoto.com) [GFDL (http://www.gnu.org/copyleft/fdl.html) or CC-BY-SA-3.0 (http://creativecommons.org/licenses/by-sa/3.0/)], via Wikimedia Commons.

Page 11. Death drop. By The original uploader was Vesperholly at English Wikipedia (Transferred from en.wikipedia to Commons.) [CC BY-SA 2.5 (https://creativecommons.org/licenses/by-sa/2.5)], via Wikimedia Commons.

Page 11. Pairs spin. By David W. Carmichael (http://davecskatingphoto.com) [GFDL (http://www.gnu.org/copyleft/fdl.html) or CC-BY-SA-3.0 (http://creativecommons.org/licenses/by-sa/3.0/)], via Wikimedia Commons.

Page 18. Death spiral. By Kevin Rushforth (Own work) [CC BY-SA 3.0 (https://creativecommons.org/licenses/by-sa/3.0)], via Wikimedia Commons.

www.ingramcontent.com/pod-product-compliance
Lightning Source LLC
Chambersburg PA
CBHW051248110526
44588CB00025B/2921